Sports Illustrated
TRACK AND FIELD: RUNNING EVENTS

The Sports Illustrated Library

Sports Illustrated

TRACK AND FIELD: RUNNING EVENTS

**By JAMES O. DUNAWAY
and the Editors of
Sports Illustrated**

J. B. LIPPINCOTT COMPANY
Philadelphia and New York

U.S. Library of Congress Cataloging in Publication Data

Dunaway, James O
  Sports illustrated track and field.

  (The Sports illustrated library)
  First ed. published in 1968 under title: Sports illustrated book of track and field: running events.
    1. Running. I. Sports illustrated (Chicago) II. Title.
  III Title: Track and field: running events.
  GV1061.D66   1972   796.4'26   79-38794
  ISBN-0-397-00889-9
  ISBN-0-397-00890-2 (pbk.)

Photographs from *Sports Illustrated*, © Time Inc.
Cover photograph: Gerry Cranham
Pages 16 and 34: Sheedy & Long
Page 64: James Drake
Page 82: David Moore–Black Star

Contents

Drawings by J. George Janes

1
Introduction

WHY do men run? Why do they race against each other? Nobody can tell you why, but both activities seem to be an instinctive part of the human temperament, present in all of us to some degree. Today, literally millions of men and women (and boys and girls) call themselves runners. Some run for glory and championships, some for the thrills of participation and competition, and some just for the fun of it. If you are one of these millions, this book is designed to help you get more out of your running.

In a way, the sport of track and field is like an iceberg. Competition is the part of the iceberg that everyone sees, while training is the much larger part below the surface. For every mile you will run in competition, you will probably run hundreds in training.

MAKE GOALS; THEN TRY TO REACH THEM

To compete effectively, you must train effectively. That means you need a goal, and a plan to reach that goal. So, first you must stop and think: What do you want out of running? What do you want to achieve?

You can—and should—set your long-range goal as high as you can imagine yourself going. Whether it is a varsity letter or an Olympic gold medal, just knowing what you are after will make it a lot easier to get there.

It may seem too much to ask to make your ultimate goal a world record or an Olympic championship. But if you are a miler, isn't it sensible to aim at eventually breaking four minutes? After all, it already has been done more than 450 times. And if you can go that far from where you are right now, why not go the rest of the way?

Of course, you are not going to do it in a year or two. It may take you five to ten years to get within striking distance of the very top. That's why you must start every year with a specific set of goals for that season and plan a training program that will make it possible to reach them. If you are a 2:10 high school half-miler, are you going to aim for 2:05 or under two minutes, or are you going to move up to the mile and try to break 4:30? The same kind of problems, different only in the times involved, face every runner, whether he is a sprinter, hurdler, middle-distance man or six-miler—and whether he is a novice or a champion.

It is not easy to know exactly what your goals should be. They must be difficult and challenging enough to make you work hard, but not so demanding as to be impossible or discouraging. A coach, a friend, a father or a brother may be able to help and advise you, but unless you yourself accept your goals seriously and believe in them they will have no value.

A sensible way out of this dilemma is to set maximum and minimum goals for yourself. First, take your wildest dreams and set them down on paper. Then, alongside, write down the least you will be satisfied with at the end of the year.

Once you have defined your objective, you can begin to plan the training program that will help you reach it. As

8

you check your progress by competition and time trials, you can modify the plan as needed, with the help of a training diary. It may be hard work at times, but it can also be a lot of fun. Because you will tend to improve as you train, you will find yourself taking pride in your improvement. You will feel yourself growing stronger, faster, tougher and smarter—and you will enjoy the feeling.

TRAINING AND THE FIVE S's

No matter what distance you run, to be successful you need certain basic qualities: speed, strength, stamina, skill and self-control. How much you need of each depends on the distance at which you race, but even a 100-yard-dash specialist needs stamina or he may be so tired from qualifying heats and the semi-finals that he can't run his best in the final. And even a marathoner needs a certain amount of speed or he may be outsprinted in the last 50 yards after leading for more than 26 miles of the race.

Training has a very simple objective: to develop these five S's in the proportion that will allow you to achieve your best possible performance at the distance in which you compete. Each training session and each exercise should be designed to improve your speed, your strength, your stamina or your skill, either separately or in combination. And every training session and every exercise should help you improve your self-control.

Only a few years ago, a naturally talented runner could go a long way by training half an hour a day, three or four days a week, for four or five months a year. Today, for runners who want to reach the level of national prominence in their early twenties, track has become a year-round sport, requiring an hour or more a day at least five days a week for almost every week of the year. For example, take Gerry Lindgren, who in 1965 set a world record for 6 miles when he was only nineteen years old. Gerry worked out two or three times a day every day, often running more than 200 miles a week, while he was still in high school. This is not mentioned to provide any young reader with a specific goal—and, in fact, many great distance runners have broken world records with far less training mileage than Lindgren—but it does demonstrate how much work a highly motivated young athlete can demand of himself.

There is no perfect training program. In fact, there seem to be almost as many opinions about the correct way to train as there are coaches and athletes. But every successful training program has certain features in common: each calls for a lot of running, each increases the amount and intensity of the training load as the athlete becomes able to accomplish more and each is aimed at the attainment of specific goals and follows a definite plan, with enough flexibility for individual differences and unforeseen circumstances.

Before we go on to study the individual events, let's get a clear understanding of what the five S's really mean, since they are the basic qualities needed by every runner.

1. *Speed* is the product of the rate of striding and the length of the stride. At full effort, a good sprinter takes about four and a half steps per second. This rate of striding, or cadence, appears to be inborn and cannot be increased appreciably. Through training, however, it is possible to lengthen the stride without affecting the cadence, thus increasing effective sprinting speed.

Sprinting speed can also be improved by increased strength, by better relaxation, by improving techniques such as starting and arm action and by eliminating waste motion in running form.

2. *Strength* is the ability to produce a high degree of muscular force against resistance in a single effort. In sprinting, each thrust of the leg driving against the track is like lifting a heavy weight. The stronger the sprinter's leg muscles, the more power and forward thrust he can obtain. Strength can be increased by resistance exercises such as weight-lifting and running up stairs.

10

3. *Stamina* is divided into two qualities, local muscular endurance and general endurance.

Local muscular endurance is the ability of a specific muscle or group of muscles to continuously perform relatively heavy work, such as sawing wood, for a long time. Developing local muscular endurance in the legs is especially important in running the longer sprints and the middle distances—races in which the leg muscles involved tend to become extremely tired although the rest of the body may still be relatively fresh.

General endurance is the over-all ability of the body to carry on moderately strenuous activity for a long period of time—the activity, in our case, being distance running at a more or less even pace. General endurance is most important to distance runners, of course, but it can be helpful to sprinters and hurdlers, too, if they compete in several events. For example, Hayes Jones, Olympic high hurdles champion, while a student at Eastern Michigan University, often ran the 100, 200, high hurdles, low hurdles and a leg on the 440 relay in a single two-hour-long dual meet. At times he broad-jumped, too. While general endurance would not have improved his performance in any of these events, it would definitely have helped to prevent a general deterioration of his performance as the afternoon progressed.

4. *Skill* is the mastery and effective coordination of the techniques involved in efficient performance of an activity —in other words, the *how* of running and hurdling properly.

5. *Self-control* is the mastery of the mental aspects of training and competition. It involves intelligence, confidence, determination, pace judgment, resistance to pain and fatigue, the will to win, concentration, planning of training and tactics, coolness under stress and other mental qualities.

To a certain extent, these are personality traits, determined by heredity and by upbringing. But, like muscles, they can be improved and strengthened by training.

11

Speaking of these qualities, Fred Wilt, who has advised many of America's best runners, says, "Regardless of what training method is used, it cannot guarantee success in racing. Training merely makes successful racing possible. A runner must also have the will to win, a subconscious desire for victory, courage, tenacity and a fierce competitive instinct to transform the racing potential provided by good training into reality."

There you have the five S's from which all good running springs. In the rest of this book, we will try to show you how to combine them most effectively for each event. There are three basic sections: (1) *sprinting*, races from 100 to 440 yards primarily concerned with speed; (2) *hurdling*, which combines sprinting with special techniques in hurdle clearance and stride control; and (3) *middle- and long-distance running*, from 800 meters and 880 yards through 6 miles and 10,000 meters. In addition, there are short chapters on warming up and weight training.

OXYGEN BALANCE AND OXYGEN DEBT

A few words must be said about what happens in the body when we run.

When our muscles perform work, such as running, they burn up body fuels, which combine with oxygen to produce the necessary energy. Oxygen from the air we breathe is taken into the blood in the lungs and pumped by the heart to the muscles.

Normally the body is in a state of *oxygen balance*, with the oxygen supplied by the blood equal to the oxygen consumed in the muscles. As we work harder, or run faster, the heart beats faster and pumps more blood (and thus more oxygen) to the muscles.

But when we run at or near top speed, the muscles need more oxygen than the blood stream can supply, even though the heart is pumping as fast as it can. Fortunately, the muscles are able to "borrow" oxygen temporarily from within the body, allowing us to keep running at close to full speed for a short time.

During this time, lactic acid is formed in the muscles in conjunction with the process that releases the borrowed oxygen. The presence of lactic acid causes the muscles to feel tired, and an excess of lactic acid prevents the muscles from working at all.

The *oxygen debt* thus created is "paid back" by the blood as soon as we stop running. This is why we continue to breathe hard—and why the heart keeps beating rapidly—for several minutes after we finish an all-out running effort. As the oxygen debt is repaid, the lactic acid in the muscles is neutralized and the heartbeat slows.

In running a 100-yard dash, nearly all the oxygen consumed is supplied through the oxygen-debt process. As the length of the run is increased and the speed is reduced, oxygen debt becomes less significant and oxygen balance becomes the vital factor.

For this reason, as we shall see, training for sprint races is very different from training for distance running.

YOUR HEART

Training for running, especially distance running, is probably the best possible exercise for the normally healthy heart, and for the entire circulatory system. Although it was once widely believed that regular, strenuous exercise could cause damage to an athlete's heart, medical and scientific studies have proved beyond doubt that regular exercise never harms the heart. In fact, quite the contrary is true. Regular exercise, and more specifically a regular program of running, makes the normal heart a stronger, more efficient muscle without any known harmful effects.

EQUIPMENT

It does not take much equipment to be a runner. All you need are a pair of warm-up shoes or sneakers for warming up and distance jogging, two pairs of spiked shoes, one for workouts and one for competition, running shorts, a tee shirt, a sweat suit, socks, and an athletic supporter.

KEEPING A TRAINING DIARY

You should keep a complete record of your workouts and competition in a diary like the one shown on page 15. You can make your own using a notebook. It will help you stick to your workout schedule and show you how you are progressing. In future years, past diaries can guide you in planning more ambitious training programs and in helping other athletes. For any serious runner, young or old, a training diary is a must.

FORMAT FOR TRAINING DIARY PAGE

DATE: (include day of week)

PREVIOUS NIGHT'S SLEEP: (hour of bedtime, hour of awakening)

PLACE OF WORKOUT: (including type and condition of surface)

PULSE RATE AT AWAKENING:

BODY WEIGHT AT AWAKENING:

WEATHER: (temperature, humidity, wind and conditions)

TIME OF WORKOUT: (hour of starting, hour of completion, any interruptions)

ACTUAL WORKOUT OR COMPETITION: (include warm-up, distance and number of interval training repetitions and recovery intervals, time of fast sections and recoveries, weight training done including weights lifted and number of repetitions and warm-down; competitive results, race description and fractional times if day of competition)

TOTAL DISTANCE RUN: (not including recovery jogs or walks)

WEIGHT

BEFORE WORKOUT:

AFTER WORKOUT:

FATIGUE INDEX

BEFORE WORKOUT:

AFTER WORKOUT:

(use a scale from 1 to 9, with 1 indicating "fresh as possible," 5 "average" and 9 "extremely tired")

COMMENTS: (any information, such as health, injuries, diet, social life or school work that might affect quality of training)

2
Sprinting

THE dictionary defines sprinting as "full-speed running." But since no one can run at absolute full speed for more than about 25 yards, we use a more accurate definition: sprinting is running a relatively short distance (up to 440 yards) at as close to full speed as possible.

As we noted, the 100-yard dash is run almost entirely on oxygen debt. Even in the 440, the amount of oxygen that the heart and blood stream can deliver to the muscles during the race is minimal—less than one fifth of the oxygen requirement.

Here are the things that are important to successful sprinting: speed of muscular contraction, stride length, strength, flexibility, reaction time, relaxation, local muscular endurance, technique and mental attitude.

The first of these qualities, speed of muscular contraction, is what makes a sprinter a sprinter. This is speed of the arm and leg muscles, and it determines the number of steps per second you can take at top speed. If you can take four and a half steps, you have a chance at becoming a successful sprinter. If you cannot, you should consider other events. Every element of successful sprinting except muscle speed can be improved by training. This can make a difference of half a second or more in your 100-yard-dash time—at least a full 5 yards.

Basically, the improvement of a sprinter involves the refinement and strengthening of his natural running movements. The object is to get rid of the wasteful movements, while making the efficient movements stronger and smoother.

This kind of polishing requires a year-round training program. Off-season training is aimed at developing strength, endurance and flexibility as well as strengthening weaknesses in technique. As the season approaches, the emphasis shifts to speed, starting efficiency, muscular endurance, and co-ordinating the over-all effort in a smooth and relaxed manner. Finally, in the competitive season, the sprinter concentrates on speed, relaxation and starting. His aim is to reach a peak of sharpness and stay there.

THE START

Of all the acquired skills of the sprinter, the start is the most important. If a slow start costs you a yard in the first steps of a 100-yard dash, you must outrun your opponent by more than a yard to win. More than likely, he will gain another yard on you due to better acceleration, giving him a 2-yard lead before the halfway mark. No sprinter can afford to give away a yard, much less 2. That is why every successful sprinter spends a lot of time taking practice starts.

The object in starting is to get into full sprinting stride as quickly as possible. Much controversy swirled around the best way to start, until Franklin M. Henry proved that the so-called "medium" start is clearly superior in producing the fastest acceleration—and thus the fastest over-all time in a sprint race.

Starting Blocks and Where to Put Them

Every sprinter should have his own starting blocks. If your team doesn't provide them and you cannot afford to buy them, you can make a passable set of blocks with two pieces of wood and some long nails or iron spikes.

The block nearest the starting line should be 15 to 18 inches behind the line. The rear block should be another 16 to 20 inches behind, so that in the "on your marks" position your rear knee is opposite your front toe. The rules require both feet to be in contact with the track.

The leg you kick a football with should be your back leg. Adjust the blocks until your body is comfortably in the positions shown for "on your marks" and "set," and then mark the blocks so that you will always start in the same position.

"On Your Marks"

Standing with your toes on the starting line, squat down and put both hands on the track in front of the line. Then, with the rear leg, reach back until the foot meets the rear block and the knee is on the ground. Next, move the front leg back until the foot is on the block and your toe opposite your rear knee. Finally, put your hands behind the line.

The arms should be shoulder width apart. Your weight should rest largely on the rear knee, plus the front foot and the hands. You should feel comfortable, relaxed and ready. Your head should be held normally and your eyes fixed on a spot about 3 feet past the starting line.

"Set"

Move the shoulders forward until they are 3 to 5 inches ahead of the hands. At the same time, raise your hips until you can feel them slightly higher than your shoulders, so

19

that your front leg is bent at a 90-degree angle and your back leg at a more open angle of about 120 degrees. You should be able to feel the pressure of the starting blocks against the soles of both feet. Your head and eyes are aimed straight ahead, still looking at that spot 3 feet down the track.

Your weight is now almost all on the hands and front foot. You have changed from a position of relaxation to one of tension, and you are ready for a good start—ready to release that tension into explosive action when the gun sounds.

But you are not listening for the gun! Instead, you are concentrating on what you are going to *do* when the gun is fired. Researchers have found that the average reaction time when concentrating on a *sound* stimulus is 0.225 second —as opposed to only 0.120 when concentrating on the *action* to be taken. That means a full tenth of a second, a yard at the end of the 100.

Of course, so many things happen at once when you start that you can only think of one action effectively. So we recommend that you think of the *arm movements* you are going to make, because that will get you moving faster than anything else—and your object, remember, is to get into full running stride as quickly as possible.

"Bang"

At the sound of the gun . . .

The arms move immediately into a vigorous alternating back-and-forth pumping motion. The arm nearest the front block slams *forward,* and the arm nearest the rear leg moves *back*—both as hard as you can. Call them the front and rear arms, and think, "*Front* arm *forward, rear* arm *back.*"

The legs at the same instant push hard against both blocks. They push *straight forward,* not up. Almost immediately the rear leg reacts in an explosive forward movement to

On your marks.

Set.

Bang!

take the first step, while the front leg continues to drive against the block low and hard.

Sprint out of the blocks with long, fast strides, *not* short, fast ones. The first step should be a natural one, but you should work to make it as long as you can without falling on your face. Make this step long by pulling the back leg through as forcefully as you can and lifting your knee as high as possible. The better you do this, the longer that first step will be. Eventually you should be able to get the first step at least 18 inches past the starting line.

The average sprinter takes about forty-five steps in the 100-yard dash. For the first twenty steps, you will be gathering speed with each step you take, and each will be a little longer than the last one.

As you come out of the blocks, you are already running. If you drive low out of the blocks, keep your knees pumping high, keep your balance and run in a straight line, you will accelerate rapidly and efficiently.

Here are some things to remember:

1. *Don't worry about body lean.* Your body leans naturally to stay in balance, and the amount of lean depends on your rate of acceleration and air resistance. Body lean is an effect, not a cause, of acceleration. If you are doing everything right, body lean will take care of itself. But if you can be seen to straighten up within a few yards of the start, this indicates you are not moving fast enough in the first few steps. To correct it, try to stay low, drive harder on each step and lift your knees higher. It may help to look at your knees for the first few strides.

In good starting, the first stride will be the shortest, the second an inch or so longer, and then each succeeding step will lengthen until full-stride length is reached, after about twenty strides.

2. *All movement should be straight ahead.* This means feet should point straight ahead; arms and legs should be worked in a straight back-and-forth action with no sideways

motion. It means *looking* straight ahead, too. And *thinking* straight ahead.

3. *Concentrate on high, straight knee action* and strong arm action. Get the most out of your own effort and don't think about your opponents. Any attention you pay to them can only be at the expense of your own performance.

4. *Your arm action should be strong and rhythmic,* in tempo with your running. Keep the elbows bent at about a 90-degree angle and try not to bring the hands higher than the shoulder or much farther back than the hips. Always try to control your arm movement so it helps you run faster, and watch out for energy-wasting excessive movement. Jumbo Elliott tells his Villanova sprinters, "Imagine you're pulling yourself up a narrow gangplank as fast as possible."

THE RACE: 100 YARDS—100 METERS

It takes a man about five to six seconds (50 to 60 yards) to reach full speed. Since this involves a series of all-out muscular exertions, one after the other without rest, it is not surprising that absolute top speed can be maintained for only a short distance. The leg muscles tire very quickly, and after running about 25 yards at top speed—at about 80 or 85 yards into the race—the sprinter starts to lose speed.

At this point it takes extra effort to avoid tying up and to continue running smoothly through the finish line.

It might seem logical to try to go faster, but you have already reached top speed so you can't go faster. In fact, your object should be to hold on to as much of your speed as possible by maintaining your running form in spite of the muscular tiredness which is attacking it.

How? Use your arms to maintain the rhythm of your running. Pump them hard. It takes extra effort to overcome fatigue. Use your legs to maintain the form of your running.

Feel yourself drive extra hard off the toes, and force yourself to lift your knees extra high.

THE FINISH

Run right through the finish as if the race were 5 yards longer than it is. Don't throw up your arms or leap at the tape. If you want to lean at the finish, lean forward from the waist on the last step before the finish line. But don't let it slow you down—or your "finish" may lose more races for you than it wins. You'll probably find you have a natural inclination to finish either straight up or leaning. Follow it.

THE RACE: 220 YARDS—200 METERS

If you try to run absolutely all-out for a full 100-yard dash, you may tie up slightly near the finish and lose a little speed. But if you try to run all-out the full distance of a 220-yard race, you will probably run out of gas and have difficulty finishing.

Instead, you divide the race into three parts: acceleration to full speed (about 60 yards), a "float" or "coast" of 100 to 120 yards, and a finishing effort of 40 to 60 yards.

Until you have reached full speed, starting and acceleration are all-out efforts, just as in the 100. Once you have arrived at top speed, you "float" by trying to keep running as fast as possible with as little effort—and as little tension—as possible.

If the idea of relaxed full-speed running sounds impossible, imagine you are pushing a big ball, five feet across and weighing 150 pounds, along the track. It takes a great deal of effort to get the ball rolling at top speed, but it takes a lot less to keep it going at top speed.

That's the float, and with practice you will find you can sustain your speed while running at less than full effort.

Olympic gold medalist Lee Evans, who has run 9.6 for 100 yards, 20.4 for 200 meters and 43.8 for 400 meters, says, "I think of running effortless. I check out every part of my body. Are my hands loose? Can I feel the skin of my face going up and down? Running relaxed postpones fatigue, yet, in the 440, the float on the backstretch is the fastest part of my race. I don't call it a float, though; I call it relaxing while you move as fast as you can. It's the same on the turn of the 220. You can't afford to slow down, but you must relax to conserve energy for the finish."

At a point perhaps 40 yards from the finish, you must gather yourself for a final effort. Once again, as in the 100, you should try to bring your knees higher and pump your arms harder to squeeze out the last bit of speed. Say to yourself, "Arms!"

It is hard to stay relaxed while putting out all this effort. It takes lots of practice—running fast 220's when you are tired and would rather quit. But it pays off in extra strength and speed just when your opponents are weakening.

Already, most world-class 220 men possess the strength and skill to run flat out for the entire distance.

Turn Running

The 220 is usually run around a full turn, and the 440 around two turns. You can't run as fast around the turn as you can on a straightaway (the difference is about four tenths of a second for a 220), but you can improve your performance on the curve.

Good turn running involves (1) running as close as possible to the inside of the lane, so you will run the shortest possible distance, and (2) leaning inward to counteract the centrifugal force generated by your body's moving at high speed around a turn.

The only way to become a good turn runner is to practice a lot of running on the turns. This can also help you escape injuries by adapting your thigh muscles to the peculiar strains involved. Don't start right out trying to run the turn at top speed, but build up to it and warm up with some medium-effort runs. Vary your practice from lane to lane; you never can tell about the luck of the draw, and you should be ready to do your best from any lane.

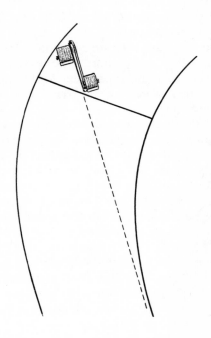

Starting on the Turn

When starting a 220 or 440 race on the turn, set your blocks on the outside edge of your lane and run in a straight line as long as possible while accelerating. This, too, should be practiced during your training sessions on running the curve.

26

THE RACE: 440 YARDS

The quarter-mile was once thought of as a middle-distance race, but today it is an endurance sprint. The race it most resembles is the 220, because a good 440 runner must have the speed to run a fast 100 and the strength to hold his speed. But the quarter requires far more strength, will power and courage than the 220.

You must work as hard as a 100-yard specialist at improving your speed and running style and at building your straight-ahead power and acceleration. And you must learn, like the 220 man, to run a curve well and to relax while maintaining as much speed as possible. But you must also add extra reserves of strength and local muscle endurance, plus the ability to plan and run your own race against temptations to panic or to be influenced by what someone else is doing.

You probably will find it best to run the quarter in three distinct parts, like the 220. The first 60 to 70 yards is spent in accelerating, just as in any sprint race. When you have reached top speed, coming off the first turn into the backstretch, you go into a float. Everything we have said about the need for relaxing while moving at close to full speed in the 220 is true here, but it is harder, because it lasts about three times as long. Then, when you can feel yourself slowing down and can see the tape, you make a last effort to reach it with a finishing surge.

Let's take up the problem of holding your speed. As in the 220, the problem is to run as fast as you can while eliminating all the tenseness you possibly can. It amounts to running fast while running easy. This kind of relaxation is probably as much mental as physical. It requires confidence as well as ability and, fortunately, both can be achieved by practice. Jim Bush, coach of John Smith who set a 440-yard world record of 44.5 in 1971, says, "Our whole fall program is devoted to running fast and relaxed. We do repeat 110's, 160's, 220's and 330's, and I time every one of them. I tell my runners to drop their shoulders on the backstretch. The object is to relax without losing speed going into the second turn. If you can do that, and if you are in top shape, the last 110 will take care of itself."

Like the shorter sprints, the quarter is usually run in lanes, so you have to learn to run your own race without watching your competitors to see how you are doing. In other words, don't worry about strategy; just cover the distance as fast as you can. To do this, you should run the first 220 yards about two seconds slower than your best time for an all-out 220-yard dash. If you go much faster, you will have trouble finishing, and if you go much slower, your over-all time will be slower than it could be. Whenever you run in a race or a time trial, be sure to have someone time you with a stop watch at the 220-yard mark.

TRAINING TIPS FOR SPRINTERS

Your starting technique should be a completely set procedure, in which one action follows another like the countdown in a satellite launching. By practicing your start over and over again, you can make good starting a habit—a conditioned reflex, as it were.

Make every practice start like the start of a real race. Get someone to give you the commands, "On your marks," "Set," "Bang," and make sure he holds you in the set position at least one full second. Run it as fast as you can, and get all the way up to top speed before you begin to slow down. In other words, run at least 50 to 60 yards.

There are two good reasons for this procedure. First, it will help you develop the kind of good starting habits that are almost automatic. Second, the all-out effort of each start builds strength and speed in the legs better than almost anything else.

To check your starting ability, have someone give you starts and time you with a stop watch at the 20-yard mark. When trying to improve your starts, *work on one thing at a time.* If you are trying to improve your arm action, concentrate on arm action until you have mastered it.

Learn from your spike marks. Study them after each all-out effort, either in practice or in a race. You will be able to see if you are running in a straight line or wavering from side to side. On the turn, they will show you how close you are staying to the line. In addition, measuring your stride length with a tape helps you check on how long your stride is—and how well you are maintaining stride length at the end of the 100 and during the float and finish of longer races.

COMPETITIVE HINTS

1. *Always run your own race.* To run your fastest requires complete concentration. Paying attention to what your opponents are doing in a sprint race never helps, and it will usually harm your performance.

2. *Use your regular warm-up.* Be sure you are ready to run your best by ending with good, hard bursts of fast running. Then go to the dressing room, replace your perspiration-soaked warm-up suit with a dry one and rest and relax until you are called to your marks.

3. *It may help you to study the starter.* It usually does not pay to waste nervous energy watching your opponents as they run their heats, but by taking easy practice starts (no need for blocks) away from the track when he is starting other races, you can observe the starter's techniques and mannerisms and get used to them. This will give you a little extra confidence when your own race comes up.

4. *Don't try to beat the gun.* All you will do is get a false start charged against you, and this just makes it that much harder to get a good start. The starter knows that his job

is to get all competitors started fairly, and most starters have too much pride to let anyone get away with a "flyer." And of course, two false starts automatically disqualify you from the race.

5. *Learn from every race.* A race is a test of what you have been practicing day after day. When it's over, analyze what you did—the things you did right *and* the things you did wrong. This can help you plan future workouts to improve weaknesses so you can do better in the next race.

6. *Make sure you are timed.* Always have someone who knows how to use a stop watch time you in every race. Even if you finish last, knowing your time can help you plan your training program.

A FINAL WORD

Keep at it. Improvement in sprinting comes slowly, but it *does* come to those who work hard. Aim at improving your best a little at a time—a tenth of a second for 100 yards per year, perhaps two tenths for the 220, and three or four tenths for the 440. If that seems too slow, project that kind of improvement eight years ahead—it could put you in the Olympic finals.

SUGGESTED TRAINING SCHEDULES FOR SPRINTERS

These workout schedules call for training from a half-hour to an hour every day. Beginners should follow them closely, but it is expected that, as you become more experienced, you will modify them to fit your own needs as shown by your performances in training and competition.

In these schedules "×" means "times." Thus "4 × 220 yards in 30 seconds" means that you should run 220 yards in 30 seconds four times. A 150-yard acceleration sprint consists of 50 yards of jogging, 50 yards of running and 50 yards of sprinting, followed by 50 yards of walking to recover. All sprints, of course, should be run at full speed.

FOR 100 AND 220 YARDS

Warm up daily before each workout as described in Chapter 5. Warm down at the end of the workout by jogging 880 yards.

Off-Season Training

Monday: a. 3 to 5 miles cross-country at easy pace.
              b. Weight training.
Tuesday: 4 to 8 × 440 yards in 70 seconds. For recovery, walk until heartbeat returns to 120 per minute (20 beats in 10 seconds).
Wednesday: Same as Monday.
Thursday: a. 4 × 220 yards in 30 seconds. Walk 220 yards after each.
              b. 10 × 150-yard acceleration sprints.
Friday: Same as Monday.
Saturday: ⎫
Sunday: ⎬   Rest or make up missed work.

Pre-Season Training

Monday: a. 6 × 60-yard sprints from blocks. Walk back for recovery. Walk 440 yards after last one.
              b. 4 × 120-yard sprints from block. Walk back for recovery. Walk 440 yards after last one.
              c. 6 × 60-yard sprints from blocks. Walk back for recovery.
Tuesday: a. 9 × 220 yards from running start. Walk back for recovery. Walk 440 yards after every third one.
Wednesday: a. 3 × 330 yards in 42 seconds. Walk five minutes after each.
              b. 6 × 60-yard sprints from blocks. Walk back for recovery.
              c. Weight training.
Thursday: a. 4 × 80-yard sprints from blocks. Walk back for recovery. Walk 440 yards after last one.
              b. 4 × 150-yard sprints around turn, with running start. Walk back for recovery.

                c. 6 × 60-yard sprints from blocks. Walk back for recovery.

Friday: a. 2 × 60-yard sprints from blocks. Walk back for recovery.

                b. 2 × 80-yard sprints from blocks. Walk back for recovery.

                c. 2 × 110-yard sprints from blocks. Walk back for recovery.

                d. 2 × 220-yard sprints from blocks. Walk back for recovery.

                e. 4 × 150-yard acceleration sprints.

Saturday: Weight training.

Sunday: Rest.

Competitive Season Training

Monday: a. 4 × 150-yard sprints from blocks. Walk back for recovery.

                b. 4 × 80-yard sprints from blocks. Walk back for recovery.

                c. 6 × 150-yard acceleration sprints.

                d. Weight training.

Tuesday: a. 2 × 330 yards in 40 to 42 seconds. Walk 110 yards after first; walk 440 yards after second.

                b. 2 × 220-yard sprints around turn, with running start. Walk 220 yards after each.

                c. 4 × 150-yard sprints around turn, with running start. Walk back for recovery.

                d. 6 × 60-yard sprints from blocks. Walk back for recovery.

Wednesday: a. 2 × 110-yard sprints from blocks. Walk back for recovery.

                b. 2 × 150-yard sprints from blocks. Walk back for recovery.

                c. 2 × 220-yard sprints from running start. Walk back for recovery.

                d. Repeat b.

                e. Repeat a.

Thursday: 6 × 60-yard sprints from blocks. Walk back for recovery.

Friday: Rest.

Saturday: Competition.

Sunday: Weight training, followed by swimming if possible.

32

FOR 440 YARDS

The workout schedule for 440-yard sprinters is substantially the same as for the 100 and 220. The only difference is this: directly after your warm-up for each workout in the pre-season period and the competitive season, take one run of 330, 440 or 660 yards at near-maximum pace without being timed.

Note: If, as a beginner sprinter, you find the training in these schedules so strenuous that you still feel tired the next day, start with half the amount and work up to the full program.

3
Hurdling

ONE of the most beautiful sights in sports is a topflight hurdles race. The runners glide over the hurdles so gracefully that it looks easy. But it isn't.

The truth is, learning to be a good hurdler is a long and difficult job. It calls for the speed of a sprinter, the agility and rhythm of a gymnast, the balance of a tightrope walker and the courage and determination of a boxer.

The most important thing to remember about hurdling is that it is *sprinting over obstacles*. This means that you must *run* over the hurdles, not *jump* over them.

The good hurdler does four things right. The first is running fast. The second is managing his steps so that he is in the right position to clear the hurdles. The third is the hurdling action itself. And the fourth is putting the first three together so they can't be seen as separate parts.

There are two main hurdles races. In the 120-yard high hurdles, the ten 42-inch hurdles are set 10 yards apart. The distance from the start to the first hurdle, and from the tenth hurdle to the finish, is 15 yards. In high school races, the hurdles are 39 inches high instead of 42.

In the 440-yard intermediate hurdles, the hurdles are 36 inches high. The distance from the start to the first hurdle is 49¼ yards (147 feet 9 inches), and the ten hurdles are 38¼ yards (114 feet 9 inches) apart. The "run-in" from the tenth hurdle to the finish is 46½ yards.

As we have said, the object of hurdling is to run over the hurdles, not to jump over them. For this reason, it is pretty hard to be a good high hurdler if you are not at least 5 feet 10 inches tall when fully grown. Of course, if you are 5 feet 7 or 8 inches in high school, you may be able to get over the 39-inch barrier reasonably well, but unless you keep growing you will find the extra 3 inches mighty tough after you are out of high school.

EQUIPMENT

In addition to track shoes and the starting blocks of the sprinter, a hurdler needs at least three hurdles to practice with. New hurdles are expensive. Often, however, you can obtain the use of hurdles without cost from your school or community recreation system either by fitting your practice schedule into time periods when they are available or by fixing up some old hurdles that might otherwise be thrown away.

If you can afford it, there are several types of practice hurdles specially designed for beginners. They protect the ankles and knees from injury by giving way easily when hit.

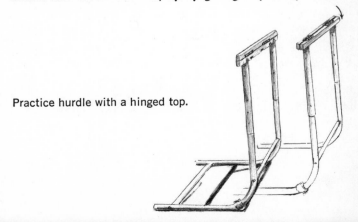

Practice hurdle with a hinged top.

If you can't afford one, you can make your own by hinging a 3-inch piece of wood to the top of the hurdle so it will fall back (as illustrated) when hit by a low lead foot or a trailing knee or ankle. Remember, though, to allow for this extra 3 inches of height by setting the hurdle at 39 instead of 42 inches high.

LEARNING TO HURDLE

Which Leg to Lead With?

This is the first thing a hurdler needs to decide. Usually the leg with which you kick a football is the leg to lead with over the hurdles, and this leg will probably feel more natural to you. If you have no natural preference, lead with your left leg. It doesn't make any difference in the high hurdles, but leading with the left leg will give you an important advantage in running the intermediates.

"Sticks and Bricks"

Unless you have already done a little hurdling, it is best to start from scratch. All you need is a track, a few bricks and three 4-foot light bamboo or wood sticks.

1. Choose a starting line and sprint five repetitions of fifteen steps.

2. Put the sticks on the track, across your lane, between the fourth and fifth, eighth, and ninth, and thirteenth and fourteenth strides, and sprint three repetitions over the sticks.

3. Put a brick, flat side up, under both ends of each stick, creating three "hurdles" 2 to 3 inches high, and sprint three more repetitions.

4. Now turn the bricks onto their narrow edges, raising the "hurdles" another inch or so, and run three repetitions at this height.

5. Next turn the bricks onto their ends and sprint three repetitions at this 8-inch height.

6. Using a second, third, and fourth brick, gradually raise the sticks to 32 inches in height, running three repetitions at each height or as many more as it takes to clear the sticks smoothly.

When the sticks reach a height of 12 inches or so, you should begin to develop the rudiments of hurdling form as shown in the action sequences on pages 41–45. Concentrate on leaning forward from the waist, bringing the lead leg up fast while shooting the opposite arm forward from the shoulder, rotating the trail leg forward from the hip when the torso has cleared the barrier and maintaining good sprinting form between the sticks. Always remember, hurdling is sprinting.

Steps to the First Hurdle

Most hurdlers take eight steps from the starting line to the first hurdle. If you are very fast or very long-legged, you may be able to get there with only seven steps, but eight is far more likely.

These first steps are important to a hurdler because they set the pattern for the whole race. Working out your own "stride plan" to the first hurdle is a matter of trial and error, but once you have worked yours out you will want to stick to it and practice continually to keep it consistent.

The take-off point for the first hurdle should be about 6½ to 7½ feet in front of the hurdle itself. Let's take 7 feet for a working figure. Since the hurdle is 15 yards (45 feet) from the starting line, the take-off point will be about 38 feet from the start.

First, without using a hurdle, set up your blocks at the starting line, measure off 38 feet and make a mark on the track. Then sprint out of the blocks at full speed for 30 yards, and walk back and check the spike marks to see where your foot landed on the eighth step. Do this several times— as many as it takes to be sure that your eighth step hits consistently at about the same spot.

If the eighth step is within 6 inches either way of the 38-

foot mark, you can use that point for your hurdling take-off. If it is short of the mark by more than 6 inches, your stride may be too short for high hurdling. If it is very much more than 6 inches past the 38-foot mark, you can adjust it either by moving your starting blocks back a little, by shortening some of your strides a little or by taking only seven steps to the take-off point. If you are long-legged enough to manage a seven-step approach, try it, adjusting your steps in the same trial-and-error way.

At this point, there is a fair chance that you will be hitting the take-off spot with the wrong foot—that is, the lead leg instead of the take-off leg—but this is no problem. It merely means you will have to reverse the front and rear legs in the starting position, thus allowing you to hit the take-off with the correct leg.

Once you have mastered the "sticks and bricks" and worked out your steps to the first hurdle, you can put up a low hurdle 15 yards from the starting line and begin serious hurdling.

Clearing the Hurdle

Remember, the hurdles is a sprint race, and the object of hurdling is to keep running while clearing the hurdles. The hurdling action is an exaggerated *step* over the barrier. It's a driving, aggressive action. You must *attack* the hurdle to clear it correctly.

Remember, too, that you should be in good condition before you start hurdling. Your conditioning should include several weeks of sprinting workouts, plus a half-hour or more of the special hurdling exercises illustrated at the end of this chapter.

Set the hurdle at 2½ feet, the lowest possible height, for your first tries. Your aim is twofold: (1) to test the accuracy of your stride pattern leading up to the first hurdle, and (2) to develop the beginnings of hurdling style while getting the feel of what you must do to clear a hurdle efficiently.

From your usual starting position, drive hard out of the blocks, just as you would in a sprint race. But because the take-off point for the first hurdle is only about 13 yards away, you can't afford the sprinter's luxury of trying for sheer speed alone. Instead, at about the fourth step you should fix your eyes on the top of the hurdle ahead.

As you reach the take-off point at sprinting speed, with the body aimed straight ahead at the middle of the hurdle, you do three things: (1) you drive the knee of the take-off leg up, lifting it high and hard, (2) you shoot the opposite arm forward straight from the shoulder and parallel with the lead leg, and (3) you *dive* forward from the waist by lowering your head and chest. All these actions should be done positively and forcefully to give you the attacking momentum you need to clear the hurdle quickly and cleanly.

As the knee of the lead leg reaches chest level, the lower leg and foot should swing out ahead, with the sole of the foot (not the toe) aimed straight ahead. This is actually a natural reaction, and it should feel natural, with the knee being slightly bent rather than locked. The opposite arm reaches toward the toe of the lead leg, and the head and chest continue to come forward so the chin is past the knee or at least above it.

As the body passes over the hurdle, the hip of the rear leg is rotated so that the trailing leg is pulled swiftly over the barrier and into the next step while the front leg is brought down fast to the track.

THE 120-YARD HIGH HURDLES

A more detailed analysis of the hurdling action is given in the action sequence that follows. Study these pictures carefully to absorb the essentials of good hurdling form.

HIGH-HURDLING FORM

In this action sequence, note how the hurdler attacks the hurdle. He dives at it, jackknifing his body forward from the waist until it is almost parallel with the thigh of his lead leg. Note also how the shoulders remain squared to the front throughout all the gyrations of the hurdling action. This helps the hurdler keep his balance, so important to maintaining sprinting speed while clearing the hurdles. The arm on the side of the lead leg is also used to help him keep his balance.

Notice, throughout the sequence, how the fingers are loosely clenched or extended, indicating the relaxation of nonessential muscles despite intense concentration on the job of clearing the hurdle.

A. The hurdler begins his approach. Eyes on the top of the hurdle, running at full speed, he carries his arms high to help him shift his weight forward. The lead leg is lifted as he comes up on his toes.

B. As the hurdler pushes off the ground, the calf of his lead leg begins to swing up from the pivot of the knee, adding to the upward and forward momentum. The body leans forward from the waist, and the arm opposite the lead leg is thrust straight ahead from the shoulder.

A

B

(continued)

Over a low hurdle, practice the action shown in the sequence on pages 41–45. When you have mastered the art of clearing one low hurdle, you can then put a second low hurdle 10 yards down the track and start practicing over a flight of two hurdles, taking three steps between the hurdles. Remember that you must *sprint* between the hurdles and *step* over them. If at first you have difficulty reaching the second hurdle with three strides, move the hurdle closer. As you become stronger through practice, you can increase the distance to the correct 10 yards.

C. The lead leg is now fully extended, with the sole of the foot aimed straight ahead (the knee is almost locked, but not quite). The opposite arm is also fully extended straight ahead, with the fingers almost touching the lead leg's toes. The upper body is bent so low that the chin is even with the knee (try bending over and doing this from a standing position—it will show you why hurdling exercises are so valuable). The trail leg is well extended, but at this point it is not doing anything except trailing, pulled along by momentum.

D. As the lead leg begins to pass over the hurdle, the trail leg begins to rotate from the hip. The knee starts to swing up and out. Note how the athlete is keeping his shoulders squared.

Here is another important tip. Whenever you practice hurdling, be sure to run full speed for at least 15 yards beyond the last hurdle. In other words, don't just clear the hurdle and stop, because this will harm your hurdling form. Instead of a flight of two hurdles, think of it as "two hurdles plus 15 yards." Since 15 yards is the distance from the last hurdle to the finish, this will also help make you a stronger finisher.

When you are doing a good job over two hurdles, the next step is to try a flight of three—plus 15 yards, of course.

E. With the body directly over the hurdle, the lead foot has already begun to descend, dropping below the plane of the top of the hurdle. The trail leg now begins to be pulled rapidly over the hurdle, continuing to rotate up and out from the hip. Note that the rear ankle is cocked slightly upward so that the toe will clear the hurdle.

F. With the body just past the top of the hurdle, the lead leg continues to come down while the trunk begins to straighten up. As the knee of the trail leg whips over the hurdle, the toe is turned up and will clear. The hurdler's eyes are already on the top of the next hurdle.

E

F

(continued)

And when you can handle three low hurdles, it is time to raise the height of the hurdle to the next level, 36 inches. This is the height intermediate hurdlers run in competition. You will find an extra 6 inches makes quite a difference, and you may want to go back to running one hurdle (plus 15 yards) to work on your form. As before, gradually step up to the flight of three-hurdles-plus-15-yards as you improve.

In the same way, when you have developed the ability to run a smooth flight of three intermediate hurdles, you then set the barriers at 39 inches, the setting used for high school high-hurdles races. And finally, if you are past high school and want to be a real high-hurdler, you'll raise the barriers to the standard high-hurdle height of 42 inches and repeat the learning process again. When you can handle a flight of three 42-inch hurdles, you'll be on your way to becoming a high hurdler.

One final point. If you find you are having trouble in

G. As the hurdler prepares to land, both his arms help him keep his balance, while the trail leg is pulled through with the knee very high. This will help make the next stride longer than it would otherwise be—a key factor in maintaining speed between the hurdles and arriving at the correct take-off point for the next hurdle.

H. As the toe of the leg reaches for the ground, the trail leg swings forward with the knee still high, in readiness for the next step. The arms, meanwhile, begin to revert to their normal sprinting action.

G

H

arriving at the correct take-off point for the second and third hurdles, you should check the length of your "getaway" stride from the preceding hurdle—that is, the first stride after your leg lands. It must be about 5 feet long; otherwise you will have to stretch too much to arrive at the take-off for the next hurdle. Lifting the knee of your trail leg high to your chest during the hurdle clearance will help lengthen your getaway stride to the necessary 5 feet.

All this takes just a few minutes to read, but it takes months to go from your first awkward clearance of a low hurdle to the running of a good three-hurdle flight of highs. Somewhere along the way you will also discover why two of the requirements for a good hurdler are courage and determination. It takes both to go back and run flight after flight of hurdles when your knees and ankles are battered and bruised—and if you hurdle, they *will* get battered and bruised.

Incidentally, if you *are* consistently hitting the hurdle

I. The hurdler, well into his next stride, reaches out with the trail leg while driving hard off the toes of the lead leg. His balance, as you can see, is perfect, resulting in a minimum loss of speed.

I

45

with the ankle of your trail leg, you can probably correct this fault by leaning forward more from the waist as you take off. If you continue to have trouble, you are probably bringing the trail leg through too soon. To correct this, consciously wait a little longer before you start to rotate the trail leg over the hurdle.

Conversely, if your lead leg is hitting the hurdle, you are probably taking off too close to the barrier, and you should adjust your stride accordingly.

PRACTICE SESSIONS

Running a full flight of hurdles is not always the best way to practice hurdling. If you are training in the off-season and have no way to check your progress, perhaps you will want to run a race-length time trial every week, and that is often enough. If you are competing regularly, you probably will not run any race-length practice flights at all.

Instead, your practice sessions will combine sprinting workouts (to increase your speed), repetitions of three- and five-hurdle flights (to improve hurdling form), and repetition workouts both with and without the hurdles (to develop the stamina to run 120 yards and clear ten hurdles at top speed).

Let's examine these three kinds of workouts in some detail.

1. *Sprinting Workouts*. To improve your sprinting speed, you have to train like a sprinter. This means plenty of short, explosive training runs of 50 to 100 yards, plus longer sprints of up to 220 yards with emphasis on relaxation while running fast. One useful variation (which combines hurdling and sprinting work in a single exercise) is to run a 30-yard sprint from the blocks over one hurdle—15 yards to the first hurdle and 15 yards beyond it.

2. *Hurdling Workouts for Form*. Improving your hurdling form is a never-ending job. For this purpose, a flight

of three hurdles is ideal; it is long enough to develop the idea of continuity (which one hurdle does not) and short enough so you can do many repetitions without becoming exhausted. Remember, always start from the starting blocks, sprint hard to the first hurdle and run that extra 15 yards past the final hurdle.

3. *Repetition Workouts for Stamina.* These can take a variety of forms. One is a series of runs over a flight of five hurdles at full speed, followed by an easy recovery jog around the track before returning to the starting line for another flight. A workout of two or three sets (six flights to a set, with a five- or ten-minute rest between sets) will help you develop the endurance to run hard over all ten hurdles without losing form over the last two or three through fatigue. If you watch many hurdles races, you will soon realize how important this is. Quite often the race is not won by the fastest hurdler but by the strongest man coming on when the leader starts hitting hurdles and slowing down over the last five.

Longer repetitions without the hurdles can also help you build stamina. Runs of 300 to 440 yards at three-quarters speed will help build both the physical and mental toughness needed to keep sprinting the full 120 yards of your hurdles race. A set of four or six, with a five-minute walk after each for recovery, is a useful example of this kind of training.

SPECIAL EXERCISES FOR HURDLERS

Hurdling requires a special muscular flexibility in the groin, hips, waist and shoulders. The exercises illustrated here should be performed every day when you are in training, and at least three times a week even in the off season. They not only will help you become a better hurdler but will also prevent many injuries. Make them a regular part of your warm-up, and never take short cuts.

A. Make a right angle between the thighs at the crotch, with each foot at right angles to the leg.

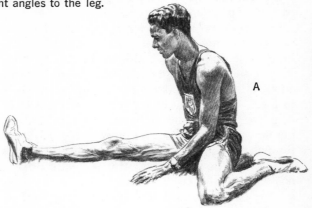

A

B. Lean forward from the waist until the chin touches below the knee of the lead leg, with the arm opposite the lead leg reaching forward straight from the shoulder and the hand touching the toes or beyond.

B

Straighten up from the waist and repeat for a total of three minutes; then reverse the legs and do another three minutes.

48

HURDLE BENDS

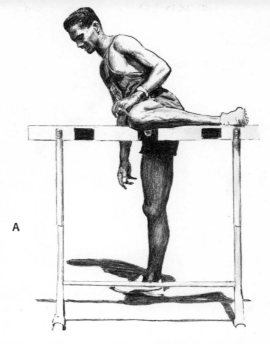

A

A. Rest the calf of one leg along the hurdle rail, with the hurdle at the 42-inch setting.

B. Bend at the waist and touch the ground with the hand nearest the hurdle. Do this for three minutes; then reverse the legs and do another three minutes.

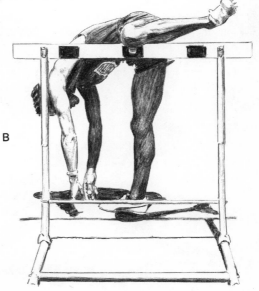

B

HIP CIRCLING

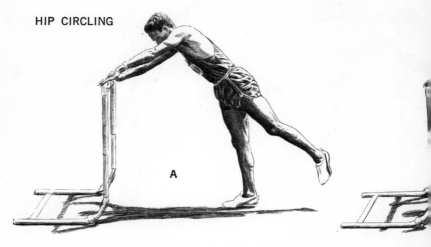

A

Place hands against a hurdle or a wall. Rotate one leg in the action of the trail leg. Be sure to lift it high enough to clear the 42-inch hurdle. Do three minutes with each leg.

SPLIT

Take a split position on the ground, with your front foot at right angles to the leg and your rear toe pointing forward. Lean forward from the waist until your chin touches the shin below the knee, using your hands for balance and support; then straighten up. Repeat for three minutes. Reverse the legs and do another three minutes.

LEAD LEG

Facing side of hurdle, stand straight with hands on end of hurdle. Kick lead leg up over hurdle from inside to outside, lifting hands to let the leg pass over the hurdle. Lean body forward from waist to imitate diving action over the hurdle. Repeat for two minutes.

TRAIL LEG

Stand alongside hurdle. Bring trail leg up behind hurdle and snap it over with a fast emphatic action, rotating hip and turning toe up as it passes over the hurdle. Repeat for two minutes.

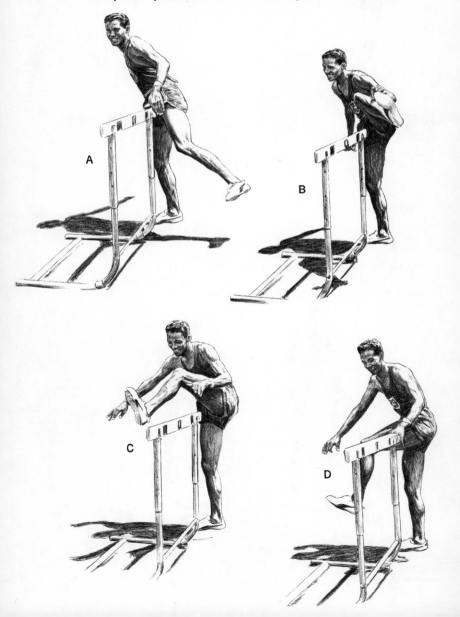

TRUNK FLEXING

Assume a split position with foot of lead leg on top of hurdle and trail foot on ground. Lean forward, stretching trunk and groin muscles; then hop forward on trail leg as hurdle bends back. Hop back to the starting position. Repeat ten times, then go through the same sequence with the legs reversed.

A

B

C

THE 440-YARD INTERMEDIATE HURDLES

In the high hurdles, once you have mastered your steps to the first hurdle and the three steps between the hurdles, the race becomes a sprint. Improvements are made chiefly by increasing sprinting speed and hurdling efficiency.

But in the intermediate hurdles, these qualities are secondary to the need for stride control, pace judgment and endurance. In fact, the specialized speed-endurance (local muscle endurance) of the half-miler probably is the most

INTERMEDIATE HURDLING FORM

The intermediate hurdler does not need to lean forward from the waist as markedly as the high hurdler, but otherwise the technique is identical. The approach is made with the arms high, and the hurdler drives hard forward and upward, lifting the lead leg high (A). Then (B and C), the calf of the lead leg swings up and the opposite arm is thrust straight ahead. As the hurdle is cleared (D), the trail leg is rotated from the hip and pulled quickly across the hurdle. As the hurdler lands (E and F), the trail leg is pulled through high and begins the next step (G). Notice the athlete's perfect balance and control through the entire flight, with the shoulders squared and the hands loose and relaxed.

needed attribute of the good intermediate hurdler, and he should include middle-distance training in his workout program.

The 440-yard hurdler must distribute his energies carefully, and must also pay careful attention to the number of steps between each hurdle.

Steps

Starting from the blocks, the first hurdle is 147 feet 9 inches away. The take-off point is 6½ feet short of the hurdle, or about 138 feet. You should be able to reach your take-off point in twenty-two, twenty-three or twenty-

four steps from the start. Only by trial and error can you determine which number of steps is right for you. Once you determine it, you should stick to this stride pattern and perfect it, practicing until you can hit the take-off right on the nose with the correct number of steps every time.

Between each hurdle you must cover 114 feet 9 inches. Since the hurdling action itself requires 11 to 12 feet, that leaves about 103 feet for running. If your stride measures 7 feet, you'll cover the 103 feet quite nicely in fifteen steps, allowing you to reach the take-off for the next hurdle with the correct foot.

If your stride is so short that you need sixteen or seventeen steps between the hurdles, you can never expect to be a fast intermediate hurdler. Most intermediate hurdlers use fifteen steps for as many hurdles as possible, changing to seventeen when tiredness starts to affect their stride length in the second half of the race.

If your stride is long enough, you may be able to use fourteen steps between hurdles, provided you can develop the rare ability to hurdle equally well off either foot. This

LEADING WITH THE LEFT LEG

This gives the intermediate hurdler an advantage when hurdling on a turn. He can stay close to the inside of his lane and is in good balance when he lands, and there is little danger of disqualification.

dual-hurdling ability allows you complete flexibility in your stride plan, since you can adjust from fourteen to fifteen, or fifteen to sixteen, steps with no loss of hurdling efficiency, and since you will always be ready to hurdle no matter which foot hits the take-off spot.

Even if you are not able to become a really effective "two-footed" hurdler, it is worth your while to learn to clear a hurdle off your "wrong" foot. When you miss your steps you will be much better off with a relatively poor wrong-foot clearance than with the almost complete loss of speed and rhythm that occurs when you have to shorten three or four steps to take off from the correct foot.

Training for the 440-Yard Hurdles

In terms of the speed at which the race is run and the endurance needed, the intermediate hurdles is a cross between the quarter- and half-mile flat races. In fact, many of the best 440 hurdlers have competed successfully at the standard indoor distance of 600 yards. The training empha-

LEADING WITH THE RIGHT LEG

This may result in the trail leg passing outside the hurdle, causing a disqualification. To avoid this, the hurdler must run well out in his lane, which forces him to cover as much as three extra yards in the race.

sis should be divided among hurdling effectively, stride practice to the first hurdle and between hurdles (using flights of four to seven hurdles), some sprint training for speed and middle-distance endurance work. Since the last two should make up an important part of your training, it will be helpful if you study carefully the chapter on middle-distance running, especially as it applies to the half-mile.

Racing Strategy

Technically, you should be able to run the 440-yard hurdles about two and a half to three seconds slower than your best 440-yard flat time. This should be your goal—but, in fact, only the best intermediate hurdlers achieve it.

To run the race well, you should strive to develop a rhythmic, even style of running that fits into your stride plan, and then develop the endurance to carry it through the entire race. As in the quarter-mile, the race is run in lanes, so you must develop a sense of pace and learn to run your own best race.

Only experience can teach you the best way to run the intermediates. Most runners prefer to run the race like a regular quarter-mile—go hard at the beginning (perhaps only two or three seconds slower than their fastest for the first 220 yards), and then hang on as well as they can at the end. Others try to run the first five or six hurdles as conservatively as possible and then finish fast over the last few hurdles.

The soundest advice we can offer is to work out a strategy that most closely fits your own abilities and then learn to race effectively using that strategy. For example, if your stride is long enough so you can manage the fifteen steps between hurdles easily at first, your natural preferences would seem to be toward a fast-finishing type of race. Conversely, if you have to run fairly fast to cover the ground between hurdles in fifteen steps, you'll probably do best when you go out fast, shifting to seventeen steps when you start to become fatigued.

SUGGESTED TRAINING SCHEDULES FOR HURDLERS

These workout schedules represent approximately one hour of training every day. Beginners are advised to follow them closely, but as you gain experience you will modify them to fit your own individual needs as reflected in training and competition.

In these schedules, "×" means "times." "5 × (start from blocks and over three hurdles). Walk back for recovery" means that you should start from the starting blocks and run over three hurdles five times, walking back to the start each time as a recovery. A "150-yard acceleration sprint" consists of 50 yards of jogging, 50 yards of running and 50 yards of sprinting, followed by 50 yards of walking to recover. All sprints should be run at full speed.

120-YARD HIGH HURDLES

Warm up daily before each workout as described in Chapter 5. Warm down at the end of the workout by jogging 880 yards.

Off-Season Training

Monday: a. 3 miles cross-country at easy pace.
            b. 6 to 10 × 150-yard acceleration sprints.
            c. Weight training.
Tuesday: a. 5 × (start from blocks and over three hurdles). Walk back for recovery.
            b. 4 × 220 yards in best 220 time plus 6 seconds. Walk 220 after each.
            c. 6 × 60-yard sprints from blocks. Walk back slowly for recovery.
Wednesday: a. 4 to 6 × 440 yards in best 440 time plus 10 to 15 seconds. Walk 3 to 5 minutes after each.
            b. 4 to 6 × 150-yard acceleration sprints.
            c. Weight training.
Thursday: Same as Tuesday.

Friday:	Same as Monday.
Saturday: }	
Sunday: }	Rest or make up missed work.

Pre-Season Training

Monday:
    a. 6 to 8 × (start from blocks and over three hurdles). Walk back for recovery.
    b. 2 × 330 yards at three-quarters full effort. Walk 5 minutes after each.
    c. Weight training.

Tuesday:
    a. 4 × (start from blocks and over six hurdles). Walk back for recovery.
    b. 2 × 220 yards in best 220 time plus 3 to 4 seconds. Walk 5 minutes after each.
    c. 6 × 60-yard sprints from blocks. Walk back for recovery.

Wednesday:
    a. 3 × full 120-yard high-hurdles course (10 hurdles). Walk 5 minutes after each.
    b. 10 × 150-yard acceleration sprints.

Thursday: Same as Tuesday.

Friday: Same as Monday.

| Saturday: } | |
| Sunday: } | Rest or make up missed work. |

Competitive Season Training

Monday:
    a. 3 × (start from blocks and over three hurdles). Walk back for recovery.
    b. 3 × (start from blocks and over six hurdles). Walk back for recovery.
    c. 3 × (start from blocks and over three hurdles). Walk back for recovery.
    d. Weight training.

Tuesday:
    a. 1 × full 120-yard high hurdles course. Walk 5 minutes for recovery.
    b. 1 × (start from blocks and over eight hurdles). Walk 5 minutes for recovery.
    c. 1 × (start from blocks and over six hurdles). Walk 5 minutes for recovery.
    d. 4 × 150-yard sprints with running start. Walk back for recovery.
    e. 6 × 60-yard sprints from blocks, concentrating on starting form.

Wednesday: a. 3 × (start from blocks and over six hurdles). Walk back for recovery.

b. 3 × (start from blocks and over four hurdles). Walk back for recovery.

c. 1 × 330 yards at three-quarters full effort.

d. 2 × 150-yard sprints with running start.

Thursday: a. 3 × (start from blocks and over three hurdles). Walk back for recovery.

b. 4 × 150-yard acceleration sprints.

Friday: Rest.

Saturday: Competition.

Sunday: Rest.

440-YARD INTERMEDIATE HURDLES

Note: Since this race is not run in high school meets, the workout schedule below is designed for college-age and older athletes.

Warm up daily before each workout as described in Chapter 5. Warm down at the end of the workout by jogging 880 yards.

Off-Season Training

Monday: a. 3 to 5 miles cross-country at easy pace.

b. 4 × 330-yard acceleration sprints.

c. 4 × 150-yard acceleration sprints.

d. Weight training.

Tuesday: a. 3 to 5 × (start from blocks over ten intermediate hurdles set at 120-yard high hurdles spacing). Walk back for recovery.

b. 10 × 150-yard acceleration sprints.

Wednesday: a. 2 to 4 × 660 yards at best 660 time plus 10 seconds. Walk 5 minutes after each.

b. 4 to 6 × 150-yard acceleration sprints.

c. Weight training.

Thursday: Same as Tuesday.

Friday: Same as Monday.

Saturday: }
Sunday: } Rest or make up missed work.

Pre-Season Training

Monday: a. 6 to 8 × (start from blocks and over first three hur-

61

dles of 440-yard hurdles race). Walk back for recovery.

    b. 6 to 10 × 110-yard run at near top speed around curve from running start. Walk back for recovery.

    c. Weight training.

Tuesday: a. 2 × (start from blocks and over first four hurdles of 440-yard hurdles race). Walk back for recovery.

    b. 2 × (start from blocks and over first six hurdles of 440-yard hurdles race). Walk 5 minutes after each.

    c. 2 to 3 × 330 yards at best 330 time plus 5 seconds. Walk 5 minutes after each.

    d. 4 to 6 × 150-yard sprints around curve from running start. Walk back for recovery.

Wednesday: a. 1 × full 440-yard hurdles from blocks. Walk 10 minutes for recovery.

    b. 1 × (start from blocks and over first eight hurdles of 440-yard hurdles race). Walk 10 minutes for recovery.

    c. 1 × (start from blocks and over first six hurdles of 440-yard hurdles race). Walk 10 minutes for recovery.

    d. 4 to 6 × 80-yard sprints from blocks. Walk back for recovery.

    e. 4 to 6 × 150-yard acceleration sprints.

Thursday: a. 2 × 660 yards at best 660 time plus 4 to 6 seconds. Walk 10 minutes after each.

    b. 4 to 6 × (start from blocks and over first three hurdles of 440-yard hurdles race). Walk back for recovery.

    c. 6 to 10 × 150-yard acceleration sprints.

Friday: a. 3 × (start from blocks and over first eight hurdles of 440-yard hurdles race). Walk 10 minutes after each.

    b. 4 × 150-yard sprints around curve with running start. Walk back for recovery.

    c. 4 to 6 × 150-yard acceleration sprints.

    d. Weight training.

Saturday: }
Sunday: }   Rest or make up missed work.

Competitive Season Training

Monday   a. 3 × (start from blocks and over first four hurdles of 440-yard hurdles race). Walk back for recovery.

	b.	2 × 330 yards at best 330 time plus 3 to 4 seconds. Walk 5 minutes after each.
	c.	4 × 150-yard sprints around curve with running start. Walk back for recovery.
	d.	Weight training.
Tuesday:	**a.**	1 × (start from blocks and over first eight hurdles of 440-yard hurdles race). Walk up to 20 minutes.
	b.	1 × (start from blocks and over first six hurdles of 440-yard hurdles race). Walk 5 minutes.
	c.	2 × (start from blocks and over first four hurdles of 440-yard hurdles race). Walk 5 minutes after each.
	d.	4 × 80-yard sprints from blocks. Walk back for recovery.
	e.	4 to 6 × 150-yard acceleration sprints.
Wednesday:	**a.**	1 × 660 yards at best 660 time plus 3 to 5 seconds. Walk 10 minutes to recover.
	b.	4 × (start from blocks and over first four hurdles of 440-yard hurdles race). Walk back for recovery.
	c.	2 × 150-yard sprints around curve with running start. Walk back for recovery.
Thursday:	**a.**	2 × 330 yards at best 330 time plus 2 to 3 seconds. Walk 5 minutes after each.
	b.	3 × (start from blocks and over first four hurdles of 440-yard hurdles race). Walk 5 minutes after each.
	c.	4 × 60-yard sprints from blocks. Walk back for recovery.
Friday:		Rest.
Saturday:		Competition.
Sunday:		Rest.

Note: If, as a beginning hurdler, you find the training in these schedules so strenuous that you still feel tired the next day, start with half the amount and work up to the full program.

4
Middle- and Long-Distance Running

WE have seen that the sprint races depend almost entirely on speed and strength, plus considerable practice and polishing on the fine points of technique—starting, arm action, turn running.

At distances over 440 yards a new factor comes into play. The importance of speed and strength starts to diminish and the need for stamina increases sharply. Instead of running all or almost all the racing distance on oxygen debt (with little or no oxygen intake), more and more must be run in a state of oxygen balance, with oxygen intake equal to consumption. Thus, increasingly, as the distance lengthens, the ability to run fast and win depends on the ability of the heart and blood stream to deliver enough oxygen to keep up with muscular activity. The more oxygen delivered, the faster will be the steady pace of the runner—that is, the more *stamina* he has.

Fortunately, we know something about how to improve oxygen-intake ability, through the use of interval training. Each time a runner creates an oxygen debt and recovers in a training run, he obtains a slight improvement in his ability to utilize oxygen effectively. By running a fairly short distance reasonably fast—say, 220 yards in thirty-two to thirty-five seconds—the pulse rate will be raised to about 180 beats per minute. This is followed by a recovery period of up to two minutes, in which the athlete jogs or walks until the pulse drops to about 120 beats per minute. Then he runs another 220. Numerous repetitions of this "run to 180, recover to 120" cycle increase the amount of blood pumped by each heartbeat (the stroke-volume) and thus improve the oxygen-intake ability. At rest, this increased stroke-volume will show itself in a much slower pulse rate. Many distance runners have a resting pulse rate of 35 per minute, and some go much lower. Ron Clarke, Australia's superb distance runner, who set 18 world records in eight events, had a resting pulse rate of 28 at the peak of his career.

Another aspect of stamina is the need for developing the body's system of capillaries. These tiny blood vessels actually deliver the oxygen to the muscles and exchange it for the carbon dioxide formed by oxidation of the fuel of muscular activity. By running very long distances at slow speeds (10 to 15 miles at a pace of six to eight minutes per mile), a runner increases the number of capillaries in his muscle fibers, which improves the speed and effectiveness of the oxygen-exchange process. This kind of training can actually double the number of capillaries in each muscle fiber.

Thus by developing both the stroke-volume (ability to move oxygen through the blood stream) and the capillary system (ability to deliver oxygen to the muscles), we can greatly increase the body's capacity for fast continuous running while remaining in oxygen balance.

The table on page 67 shows the approximate proportions

of speed and stamina needed for varying distances from 100 yards to the marathon. Since the table is chiefly based on the runner's oxygen requirements, it can be used as a rough guide for determining the relative proportion of training time to be spent on speed and endurance workouts.

Note that the half-miler still needs more speed than stamina. About two thirds of his total oxygen need during a race can be met by oxygen debt, leaving one third that must be supplied during the race. Thus his training would emphasize speed work for two thirds of the time and endurance one third of the time. The miler supplies about half the oxygen he needs during a race, so his training efforts would be divided about fifty-fifty between speed and stamina. And so on up to the marathoner, who must run 26 miles in a state of oxygen balance, supplying almost all his own oxygen needs during the race, and who accordingly trains almost exclusively for endurance.

SPEED VS. STAMINA NEEDED FOR VARIOUS DISTANCES

Distance	Speed	Stamina
100 yards	95%	5%
220 yards	90%	10%
440 yards	80%	20%
880 yards	65%	35%
one mile	50%	50%
two miles	40%	60%
three miles	20%	80%
six miles	10%	90%
marathon (26 miles)	5%	95%

TYPES OF TRAINING

Interval Training—Endurance, Speed, Repetition Sprints

Interval training is by far the most useful and versatile method for improving the performance of middle- and long-distance runners.

Developed by trial and error over a period of years, interval training and its successes have inspired much scientific research. It has been found that there are actually several different kinds of "interval training," each with special benefits for the runner.

We have already seen how alternate periods of fast and slow running can be used to improve over-all endurance. By varying the speed of the run, the distance of each fast run, the number of repetitions and the recovery interval, interval training can also improve the runner's speed and his ability to sustain speed over increasingly longer distances.

1. *Endurance Interval Training.* As we noted in the preceding pages, the purpose of endurance interval training is to increase the amount of blood pumped by the heart with each stroke. To do this, you do not have to run at full speed, merely fast enough to bring the pulse up to 180 (or 30 beats in ten seconds). Generally you should run six to ten seconds slower than your fastest time for 220 yards with a running start. For most athletes, running 220 yards in thirty-two to thirty-five seconds, or 440 yards in seventy to seventy-five seconds, will do the job. It is easy enough to check your pulse at the end of a 220 and adjust your speed to what is needed. Naturally, as your condition gradually improves, you will find it necessary to increase the speed slightly from time to time. Recovery, of course, should be the time it takes for your pulse rate to drop to 120 per minute, or 20 beats in ten seconds—probably about one and a half minutes and no more than three.

But the main change as you improve in endurance will be toward a greater number of repetitions of the basic distance of 220 and 440 yards. At first, you will start out with as few as ten repetitions of the distance, but you will find that soon you will be able to increase the load (and if you are serious about running you will want to) to twenty and then to thirty or forty. When you are doing this many, it is sensible to break them into "sets" of ten each and get a complete rest by walking for five minutes between sets.

One extra benefit you will get from these workouts (and from all interval training) is a sense of pace judgment. You will find yourself able to tell how fast, to within less than a second, you are running a quarter-mile, a very helpful ability when you are racing.

2. *Speed Interval Training.* This type of interval training is especially helpful for half-milers and milers. It develops the special kind of speed-endurance (known as local muscle endurance) that enables middle-distance runners to sustain a pace close to their top speed for several minutes. It is also helpful to distance runners in developing a strong finishing kick.

Speed interval training is done at racing speed or slightly faster over distances from 110 yards to perhaps as much as 880 yards. The recovery is not as complete as in endurance training, because the purpose is to accustom the leg muscles to hard work without complete removal of lactic acid. It is a kind of "vaccination" in which the runner's muscles build up a tolerance for continued activity past the point at which he ordinarily would not be able to keep running.

Your speed should be three to five seconds slower than your best time for 220 yards with a running start. At first, the recovery interval should consist of walking or jogging until your pulse returns to about 120 per minute.

A runner who does endurance interval training by running repeats of 220 yards in thirty-two seconds with a ninety-second recovery interval probably will run his speed interval training repeats in twenty-eight to thirty seconds, with a recovery interval at first of up to two or three minutes of jogging or walking. As you progress, you will be able to make the recovery interval shorter—and you should, so as to get the fullest benefit from this kind of workout. Of course, this is hard work, and you can't do as many repetitions as in endurance training.

Speed interval training should also be used by the runner to work on the rhythm and relaxation of his racing style. The last couple of a series of fast quarter-miles will impose

69

a strain something like that met in the last lap of a race, where running form and relaxation are hard to maintain. Create a race situation in your mind and then work to keep moving fast and smoothly without tightening up. This can make a positive contribution to your racing abilities.

3. *Repetition Sprinting.* The best way to improve speed is to run at or near top speed. Because sprinting is an all-out effort, the muscles involved develop increased strength only when they are worked close to their limits. In the same way that weight lifters develop muscles by lifting the maximum weight possible, runners develop leg power (and thus speed) by running as fast as possible.

In speed training, the athlete runs as fast, or nearly as fast, as he can for short distances up to 220 yards. The recovery interval is as long as it takes for complete freshness to return, perhaps as long as five or ten minutes.

To a three-miler or six-miler, spending half an hour doing repeated 100-yard dashes may seem like a complete waste of time, and certainly such a workout is not recommended as a steady diet. But it can prove a very good investment indeed if the three-miler finds another three-miler alongside of him 100 yards from the end of a race.

Sprint training has two other virtues. First, anything that helps improve basic speed is worthwhile to a runner. After all, *speed* is what running is chiefly about, and improving basic speed gives a great psychological boost even to a marathoner. Second, a little speed training provides added *interest* to the distance runner's training grind.

Long-Run Training

As mentioned in the first part of this chapter, very long runs at slow speeds (between six and eight minutes per mile) help develop the capillary network and thus help improve the body's ability to utilize the oxygen in the blood. In addition, long runs help develop general endurance and are an extremely effective way of keeping body weight down.

70

In other words, continuous long runs of 6 to 20 miles once or twice a week are a perfect and necessary complement to interval training.

Although the idea of this kind of running is to get strong by taking it fairly easy, you can vary your even pace by running a little faster on the hills, and you probably will want to pick up the pace for the last mile or two, accelerating gradually to a fast finish over the last quarter-mile. Keep yourself honest by deciding how far you are going to run beforehand (or for how long a time), and stick to it.

Just one caution: during the hot months, do your long runs either early in the morning or in the cool of the evening. A 15-mile run in the heat of the day carries with it an unnecessary risk of sunstroke, heat exhaustion or excessive dehydration. Incidentally, if you have trouble with chafing, a little Vaseline applied to the affected area before you start running will prevent it.

Fartlek Training

Fartlek is a Swedish word which means "speedplay," and speedplay pretty well describes what Fartlek is. It was popularized by Gosta Homer, former Swedish Olympic coach, to make training more natural and enjoyable, as opposed to the rigidly planned daily workouts then popular.

Fartlek training is done away from the track. It involves continuous running at varying speeds, if possible over a soft springy surface like the pine-needle paths of a Swedish forest. A path in the woods, a golf course, a beach, a country road or a city park will do. There should be a hill or two to provide uphill and downhill running.

The essence of a Fartlek workout is *continuous movement* and *variety*, and many athletes have developed their own favorite schedules of Fartlek work. Here are a couple of programs to give you an idea.

First, Gosta Homer's own recipe, as related to Cordner Nelson of *Track and Field News* in 1949:

71

The athlete should train from one to two hours each day, according to the following schedule:

1. Warm up with easy running for 5–10 minutes.
2. Steady, fast running for ¾ to 1¼ mile (4–6 minutes).
3. Fast walking for about 5 minutes.
4. Easy running or jogging, broken up by windsprints of 50–75 yards, repeated until you feel a little tired.
5. Easy running with three or four quick steps now and then. These steps would be like the sudden speeding up of a runner during a race when someone tries to pass him.
6. Full speed uphill for 175 to 200 yards.
7. Fast pace for 1 minute following this trial of strength (the uphill run).

Homer went on to add: "The above workout can be repeated until the end of the time scheduled; but every athlete must remember that he must not feel *tired* but rather stimulated after the training. Always finish the training by running on the track from one to five laps, depending on what distance you run in competition." (This is pace work, run at racing speed, covering one quarter to one half of your racing distance.)

Fred Wilt says: "Although there are infinite varieties of Fartlek, a typical example might be:

1. Jog 10–15 minutes at a speed of 8–10 minutes per mile, covering 1½–2 miles as a warm-up.
2. Perform 5–10 minutes of vigorous calisthenics.
3. Run at a fast, continuous speed for 4–6 minutes, covering ¾ to 1¼ miles.
4. Walk for 3 to 5 minutes.
5. Jog about 1 mile in 8 minutes, doing 4–6 sprints of 75–110 yards enroute.
6. Sprint uphill 150–200 yards. If no hill is available, run 660 yards at near maximum speed.
7. Jog one mile, taking very short, fast 5–10 yard rushes or bursts of speed enroute.
8. Walk 10 minutes.
9. Then, on a track, road, or other level area where one can achieve good speed, run 2–4 × 440 yards at racing speed, jogging 440 yards after each. Time with a stopwatch if possible.

72

10. Jog one mile in about 10 minutes to complete the workout."

As you can easily see, Fartlek is a kind of rough-and-ready combination of interval training and continuous long running. It has proved a successful training method for many athletes because it enables them to do a lot of running and *enjoy* it.

Only one word of caution. Fartlek does require self-discipline to avoid its becoming more than a long, slow run. Remember that Fartlek means "speedplay," and keep the workout honest with those bursts of speed and occasional long segments of hard running.

PUTTING TOGETHER A TRAINING PLAN

The five types of training described on pages 67–73 contain all the ingredients needed for success at distances from 880 yards and up. Now the question is: How do you put them together for the best results?

The answer is different for each runner, and it depends on three factors: (1) the length of the race or races you are training for, (2) the season of the year in which you are currently training, and (3) your own personal feelings, strengths and weaknesses.

Let's take our three factors one at a time. First, the length of the race. If you are a half-miler, you can see by the chart on page 69 that about two thirds of your training efforts will be spent in sprinting and speed interval training, and one third on endurance training. If you're a miler, the division is about fifty-fifty, and for the longer distances, the proportion of endurance-type training increases quite sharply, up to nearly 100 per cent for marathoners.

Second, the season. It is convenient to divide the competitive year into three parts—off-season, pre-season and in-season. The off-season, which starts for most runners in late summer and extends through the fall (and perhaps the winter), is the time to emphasize endurance work. It is a time for strengthening yourself, building up a base for faster work in the future with a good volume of low-intensity training. As the time for competition draws closer, a shift is made toward faster training, with decreasing emphasis on endurance. Then, as the competitive season progresses, almost all workouts are devoted to fast training and correcting weaknesses discovered in races.

Third, yourself. Every runner has his strengths and weaknesses, his likes and dislikes and his favorite ways of training. Olympic 5,000-meter champion Bob Schul did practically all his training on the track, doing repeated interval work at distances from 110 to 440 yards. Olympic 10,000-meter champion Billy Mills did almost all his training *off* the track, using long, hard runs and plenty of Fartlek but virtually no interval training as such. Both ways seem to produce results. So it is up to you to work out the kind of training program that will do you the most good. As long as you work hard and put in the mileage, the results should take care of themselves.

TACTICS

Australian coach Franz Stampfl has very neatly summarized the object of racing: You run to win; if you can't win, you try to finish second, and if you can't take second, third; and if you can't win a medal, you at least aim to do better than you ever have.

In training, you start every session with a plan. In racing, a plan is even more important. And before the plan comes the goal.

Your goal can be to win, or to run a certain time, or to set a record, or perhaps to score as many points as possible while saving something for another race. This is something you will decide, probably with your coach. Some of the factors to consider are: the time of year, your condition, the abilities and condition of the competition, the importance

74

of the race, how many other races you will have to run on the same day (or have run).

You cannot decide how the race is going to be run unless you are by far the best runner in the field. But you *can* plan many things. Taking your opponents' known strengths into consideration, you can form an optimum strategy for running your best race and for winning.

Basically, there are two ways to win a race. You either run in front, all or much of the race, or you come from behind at the end of the race.

Since you are an amateur, you can forget about what the sports writers, the hangers-on and the fans say. You are under no obligation to please them. You are not out to make an interesting race of it—you are out to do your best as *you* see it.

So let's be logical. If you are going to be a front runner, your objective is to *stay* in front *all the way.* Running in front has its advantages. You decide the pace, and you can make it as fast as you want. You can also vary it. You don't have to worry about being boxed. Until the final portion of the race, the leader can break contact by choice and force the others to run his way. He stays out of trouble too.

But for many runners, the disadvantages of front running are great. Setting the pace in a fast race carries a psychological burden of "doing the work" for the whole field, and sometimes, when running into the wind, the leader actually does serve as a windbreak for runners behind him. Most important, he cannot keep an eye on the runners behind him and is vulnerable to being passed without warning and finding himself suddenly several yards behind.

A front runner, of course, does not have to lead the entire race. But a runner who wins from in front will, in fact, probably lead for at least the last half of the race. He has no intention of setting a pace for others; his object is to put as much distance as possible between himself and the opposition.

His real opportunity often comes in the third quarter of a race—before the "kicker" commits himself.

To win, a front runner must either (1) break contact with the rest of the field, (2) hold off the finishing moves of those behind him with a sprint of his own, (3) set such a fast pace that runners who could normally outkick him have nothing left or (4) use surprise tactics to upset the usual tactics of the competition.

If you feel that a fast race is needed, you probably will have to set the pace. At least, you will have to be ready to.

Because only one man can lead, running from behind is obviously the tactic most runners will use most of the time. It is a lot easier to follow a pace than to set it, no matter how fast. A runner can say to himself, "If he can do it, I can do it." While keeping within striking distance of the front runner, he can easily adjust to variations of pace. Best of all, of course, he has the advantage of surprise when he makes his move. By accelerating suddenly, he can burst past the leader and open a gap of several yards before a counterattack can be made.

Great runners have used every tactic. Some, like Peter Snell and Ron Delany, with supreme confidence in their abilities to keep up with any pace and outkick the leaders, virtually never took the lead in a major race before the last half-lap. Others, including Herb Elliott and Ron Clarke, generally preferred to apply the pressure from in front.

You probably will develop a preference for leading or following based on your temperament, but you will be a better runner if you learn to race both ways. The best mental attitude you can bring to an important race is the confidence that you are in condition to win; but the next best is the confidence that you can handle any kind of tactical opposition from anyone in the field.

Jim Ryun has demonstrated this kind of confidence. In 1967 he set his world record in the mile (3:51.1) by leading and pacing himself from start to finish. In a 1,500-meter race that same year, he didn't take the lead until the last

76

220 yards, outkicking his opponent Kipchoge Keino of Kenya and setting another world record (3:33.1). "If it's a slow race," says Ryun, "I go ahead and lead, but if the pace is fast, I'd rather follow and kick at the end."

It is especially important for the "sitter" to learn how to handle the pace-setting chores. Use races of lesser importance to gain experience in running and winning from the front. It may well come in handy in an important race where a slow-slow pace forces you to the front at the halfway mark. Certainly, you can never get too much experience in racing tactics.

For championship-class runners, skill and confidence in tactics are often the determining factors. The classic case is perhaps the Olympic 10,000 meters race of 1956. In June of that year Vladimir Kuts of Russia, a front runner par excellence, led Gordon Pirie of England for almost all of a fast 5,000 meters. So fast was it that both broke the world record, Pirie's finishing speed carrying him to a 25-yard victory over the last 300 yards of the race.

In November at Melbourne, Kuts knew he could not again afford to set a fast and even pace for Pirie. "I knew the English runners would follow hot on my heels provided that I did not change my tactics, and that they would be able to win at the end with their superior speed."

So Kuts drastically altered his style. Instead of setting a fast, steady pace in the Olympic 10,000 meters, he alternated his regular rhythm with bursts of near-sprinting speed, forcing Pirie to run a different (and unexpected) kind of race. With four laps to go, Kuts' attacking tactics finally "broke" Pirie, and Kuts was alone, nearly 100 yards in front, as Pirie faded to eighth. Kuts went on to win the 5,000 meters as well.

Kuts had spent four months practicing his new strategy. During his bursts of extra speed, Kuts experienced as much pain as any of his opponents, but he knew he could do it because he had done it scores of times in workouts. All his opponents could do was try to keep up, meanwhile wondering: What will this crazy Russian do next? As a result, Kuts inflicted more damage on the others than on himself, and his prize was a great one—two Olympic gold medals.

Four years later Murray Halberg of New Zealand stole the Olympic 5,000 meters from a closely matched field with a brilliant and surprising tactical move. With three and a half laps to go, and the other runners in the field thinking ahead toward the final lap instead of concentrating on the race at that moment, Halberg made his move. Even from the stands, one could see the shock and indecision of the other leaders as Halberg moved away from them. Before any of them could respond, Halberg had taken a 20-yard lead, and he saved enough of it over those agonizing last two laps for a 7-yard victory and an Olympic gold medal.

What kind of tactics are best? What makes one man a consistent front runner and another a sitter? It seems to be a question of what feels right to the individual. Some runners enjoy being out in front, in charge of the race and dictating the tempo of the proceedings. Others, not having the finishing kick necessary to win from behind, are forced to become front runners and tactical experts if they are going to have a chance.

Unless you are a world-class runner, I think you are better off trying to run close to your best time in every important race. It may cost you some victories in the short run, but it will make you a faster, better and more respected runner in the long run.

SUGGESTED TRAINING SCHEDULES FOR MIDDLE-DISTANCE AND DISTANCE RUNNERS

Because middle-distance and distance runners vary more widely in their abilities and needs than sprinters and hurdlers, these suggested workout schedules are much more loosely drawn than those for sprinters and hurdlers. They should be used as guides, not as ironclad directions. They indicate in a general way the types of workouts that should help you improve your performance, but it is up to you to design the specific program you will follow.

It is suggested that each month you write down your program for the next four weeks, based on the previous month's training and/or competitive results.

These schedules are based on an hour to an hour and a half of training per day, six days a week. Any less than an hour a day is probably not enough, and you can undoubtedly profit by increasing your workouts to two hours a day if this is not too tiring, or by adding a half-hour or more of steady, even-pace running in the morning to your daily program.

If you are fifteen years old or under, three or four days a week of training is sufficient. If you are sixteen or seventeen, you may want to work out five days a week instead of six.

Workouts should leave you tired but not exhausted. If you still feel tired at the start of the next day's workout, it doesn't hurt to take a light workout or an extra day of rest, as long as you don't make it a habit.

OFF-SEASON TRAINING

(Three to six months; emphasis is on endurance)

All Distances

2 days per week:	One hour Fartlek, plus weight training as in Chapter 6.
2 days per week:	Endurance interval training. Run 220 or 440 yards fast enough to increase the heartbeat to 180 per minute; then jog an equal distance slowly enough to bring the heartbeat down to 120; repeat. Run sets of eight to ten, walking a lap slowly between sets. The fast runs should add up to three to five times your racing distance.
2 days per week:	Easy 1½-hour continuous run.
1 day per week:	Rest.

PRE-SEASON TRAINING

(Two to three months; emphasis shifts toward speed)

Half-Milers

3 days per week: Speed interval training. Gradually replace Fartlek and most endurance interval training, increasing from one day of speed interval training the first week to three the third or fourth week. Run 220 yards at race speed or faster, with recovery jogs of 2 to 3 minutes, gradually speeding up the fast portions and reducing the recovery intervals to about 1 minute as you are able. Run sets of four, with 5 minutes of walking between sets. Include 15 minutes of repetition sprinting or acceleration sprints in each workout.

1 day per week: Endurance interval training, finishing with 15 minutes of repetition sprinting or acceleration sprints.

1 day per week: Repetition sprinting. Start with two or three laps of 150-yard acceleration sprints (jog 50 yards, run 50 yards, sprint 50 yards, then walk 50 yards for recovery). Then sprint various distances from 50 to 150 yards, walking back slowly for recovery, in sets of four. Take 5 minutes of walking rest between sets.

2 days per week: Weight training in addition to workout.

Weekends: Easy 1½-hour continuous run one day. Rest the other day.

Milers

2 days per week: Endurance interval training, finishing with 15 minutes of repetition sprinting or acceleration sprints.

2 days per week: Speed interval training. Run 220 or 440 yards at race speed or faster, with recovery jogs of 2 to 3 minutes. Gradually speed up the fast portions and reduce the recovery intervals as you are able.

1 day per week:	Repetition sprinting as for half-milers.
2 days per week:	Weight training in addition to workout.
Weekends:	Easy 1½-hour continuous run one day. Rest the other day.

Three-Milers

4 days per week:	Endurance interval training. On two days, finish with 15 minutes of repetition sprinting or acceleration sprints. On the other two days, finish with weight training.
1 day per week:	Easy 2-hour continuous run.
1 day per week:	Speed interval training, as for milers.
1 day per week:	Rest.

COMPETITIVE SEASON TRAINING

(Emphasis is on speed, maintaining condition, correcting weaknesses; hard training early in week, tapering off toward end)

Half-Milers

2 days per week:	Speed interval training (Mon. and Wed.).
1½ days per week:	Repetition sprinting (full day Tues., half-day Thurs.).
Day before competition:	Rest or half-hour of jogging, if preferred.
Day after competition:	Up to 1 hour of jogging or easy cross-country run.

Milers

2 days per week:	Speed interval training, plus 15 minutes of repetition sprinting or acceleration sprints.
1 day per week:	Endurance interval training, plus 15 minutes of repetition sprinting or acceleration sprints.
1 day per week:	Repetition sprinting.
Day before competition:	Rest or half-hour of jogging, if preferred.
Day after competition:	1 hour of jogging or easy cross-country run.

Three-Milers

3 days per week:	Endurance interval training, plus 15 minutes of repetition sprinting or acceleration sprints.
1 day per week:	Speed interval training.
Day before competition:	Rest or jogging, if preferred.
Day after competition:	1½-hour easy cross-country run.

5
Warming Up Before You Work Out

A good warm-up loosens the muscles, sinews and joints and alerts the circulatory system to prepare you for the hard work of a training session or a race. Even more important, a good warm-up *helps prevent injuries.*

Just before the 1956 Olympics in Melbourne, two-time gold-medal-winner Lee Calhoun was talking about the value of a warm-up. Lee would spend more than half an hour every day warming up, doing stretching, bending, twisting and loosening exercises. He was asked, half jokingly, if he weren't overdoing it a little.

"Maybe so," Lee answered. "But I've never had an injury, and my warm-up is why. I wouldn't *think* of practicing a start, or running hard, or clearing even one hurdle until I've done my full warm-up. If you want pulled muscles, just take a short warm-up."

In other words, *never work out or compete without a thorough warm-up.* The only exception to this rule is when your entire workout consists of jogging and easy running.

Here is a 20- to 25-minute warm-up routine that will get you ready for anything. Sprinters and hurdlers need the full routine. Middle- and long-distance runners can cut the exercises in half, but not the running.

1. Jog four laps. First lap, very slow (3 minutes). Second lap, slow (2½ minutes). Third lap, 2 minutes. Fourth lap, jog 50 yards, run 50, all the way around, last 50 full speed.

2. Arm swings, 30 seconds each arm. Arm fully extended. Swing loosely from the shoulder in full circles.

ARM SWING

TRUNK BEND

A   B   C

3. Trunk bends, 1 minute. Feet apart, hands on hips. Bend from waist and touch ground with hands without bending knees. Straighten up, put hands on hips and lean back from waist.

4. Hand bounces, 30 seconds. Feet apart. Bending over, "bounce" hands between ground or floor and knees. Try to touch entire palm of hand to ground.

HAND BOUNCE

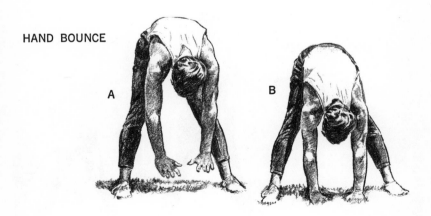

A   B

HULA HOOPS

5. Hula hoops, 1 minute. Hands on hips, feet apart. Rotate hips in hula hoop motion. After 30 seconds, reverse direction.

6. Wood choppers, 1 minute. Hands together over head, feet apart. Bend over and touch both hands to one foot, then straighten up and repeat to other foot.

WOOD CHOPPER

SIDE WINDER

7. Side winders, 1 minute. Feet wide apart (4 feet). Bend one knee and lean body sideways to put full weight on that leg, stretching other leg. Repeat on other side.

8. Bicycling in air, 30 seconds. Lie on back, hands under hips. Cycle vigorously with legs.

9. Leg overs, 1 minute. Lie on back, hands under hips. Raise legs straight up, then touch ground behind head with one leg, then with the other. Return to start and repeat.

BICYCLING IN AIR

LEG OVER

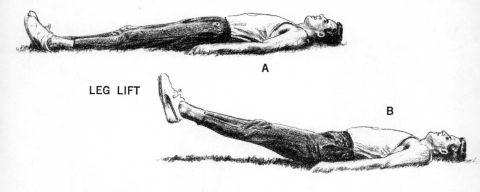

LEG LIFT

10. Leg lifts, 1 minute. Lie on back. Raise legs about one foot off ground, and hold for a slow count of 10.

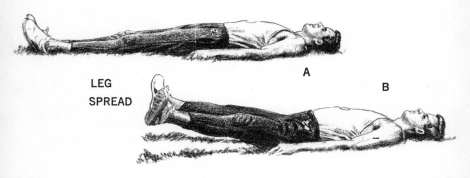

LEG SPREAD

11. Leg spreads, 30 seconds. Lie on back. Raise legs slightly off ground and spread sideways as wide as they will go—about 4 feet.

12. Hurdling exercise, 2 minutes, 6 each side. Pump five times.

GROUND HURDLING

HALF SQUAT–THRUST BOUNCE

A

B

13. Half squat–thrust bounces, 1 minute. Squatting position, feet slightly apart, hands on ground in front of them. Thrust one leg back straight and bounce up and down so you can feel the muscles stretch. After 30 seconds, reverse the legs.

14. Running in place, 1 minute. Get up on your toes, use high knee action and pump hard with arms.

RUNNING IN PLACE

LEG KICK

15. Leg kicks, 30 seconds with each leg. Kick as high as you can.

16. Run two laps, alternately running and jogging 50-yard segments, and gradually increasing the speed of the running segments.

Sprinters and distance runners can go right into the workout or take a short rest (5 to 10 minutes).

Hurdlers should continue with 15 to 30 minutes of special hurdling exercises; 15 minutes is the absolute minimum.

6
Weight Training

WE have said repeatedly that the best training for running is *running*. But there comes a time for every runner when an hour or so of weight lifting a week will do him more good—and make him a better runner—than another hour of running.

For the sprinter and hurdler, weight training can provide extra strength and explosiveness in the muscles used for starting and running at top speed. For the middle-distance and distance runner it can add upper body and abdominal strength to complement the strength and endurance of the legs.

Besides giving you certain kinds of strength that no amount of running can give, weight training adds interesting variety to your training schedule.

Most school, college and YMCA gyms have the simple weights needed for these exercises. When starting, ask the instructor or person in charge to show you the correct way to lift weights and to watch you and make sure you are doing the exercises correctly.

If no guidance is available, remember these three rules: (1) keep your feet close to the weight when you pick it up, (2) keep your head up and look straight ahead, and (3) (most important) bend the *knees* and keep your back straight when lifting weights from the floor.

How much should you lift? The weights you lift should be fairly heavy, because *strength* is built by lifting heavy weights a few times, as opposed to lifting light weights many times, which builds *endurance*. Generally speaking, you should lift a weight that allows you to do an exercise at least five times but no more than ten times. When you can repeat a lift ten times without stopping, add 5 or 10 pounds to the weight. Suggested starting weights are given in the Lifting Program on page 96.

MILITARY PRESS

A

B

Each group of exercises is arranged so that one set of muscles is resting while another set is working; so you can perform the entire sequence with a minimum of time lost in recovery. After warming up well, do the exercises in order, one after the other, with no rest period between exercises. Then rest for three to four minutes and repeat the sequence. Take another three- to four-minute rest and do the exercises a third time. On this third sequence, do as many of each exercise as you can, up to ten. If you can reach ten easily, it is time to increase the amount of weight you are lifting.

ARM CURL

A   B

STRAIGHT-ARM PULLOVER

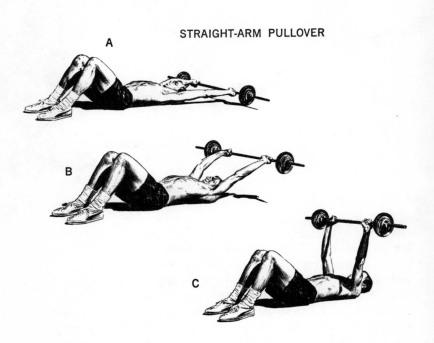

A

B

C

C

TOE RAISE

A

B

A

SIT-UP

B

C

In the off-season, lift three times a week. As the season nears and running becomes more intense, cut down to twice weekly.

SUGGESTED LIFTING PROGRAMS

FOR SPRINTERS AND HURDLERS (UP TO 440 YARDS)

Warm-up: 10 minutes of calisthenics.

1. *Military press,* ⅓ body weight. Five repetitions.
2. *Half squat,* body weight. Five repetitions.
3. *Straight-arm pullover,* ⅙ body weight. Five repetitions.
4. *Arm curl,* ⅓ body weight. Five repetitions.
5. *Toe raise,* ½ body weight. Five repetitions.
6. *Sit-ups,* one minute. Start with 15 per minute, increasing to a maximum of 30 per minute. Then add 5-pound weight behind neck while maintaining rate of 30 per minute.
7. *Twenty-step stair climb* at full speed; walk down. Five repetitions. (To increase difficulty, use leg or body weights or carry weights in hand.)

Repeat the sequence three times. Rest a few minutes before each sequence. Always be careful when lifting weights.

FOR MIDDLE- AND LONG-DISTANCE RUNNERS

Warm-up: 10 minutes of calisthenics.

1. *Arm curl,* ⅓ body weight. Five repetitions.
2. *Sit-ups,* as in 6 above. Fifteen to thirty per minute.
3. *Military press,* ⅓ body weight. Five repetitions.
4. *Half squat,* body weight. Five repetitions.
5. *Straight-arm pullover,* ⅙ body weight. Five repetitions.

Repeat the sequence three times, resting between each sequence.